KAWHI LEONARD

BASKETBALL SUPERSTAR

BY TODD KORTEMEIER

First Edition
First Printing, 2020

Book design by Jake Nordby
Cover design by Jake Nordby
Photographs ©: Frank Gunn/The Canadian Press/AP Images, cover, 1, 23, 25, 27, back cover; Wilfredo Lee/AP Images, 4; Tony Gutierrez/AP Images, 6; Richard Hartog/Los Angeles Times/Getty Images, 8; Ed Andrieski/AP Images, 11; Julie Jacobson/AP Images, 13; Bill Kostroun/AP Images, 14; Pat Sullivan/AP Images, 17; Eric Gay/AP Images, 19; Jonathan Hayward/The Canadian Press/AP Images, 20-21, 30; Yuliyan Velchev/Shutterstock Images, 24; Red Line Editorial, 29

Press Box Books, an imprint of Press Room Editions.

Library of Congress Control Number: 2019944757

ISBN
978-1-63494-145-7 (library bound)
978-1-63494-146-4 (paperback)
978-1-63494-147-1 (epub)
978-1-63494-148-8 (hosted ebook)

Distributed by North Star Editions, Inc.
2297 Waters Drive
Mendota Heights, MN 55120
www.northstareditions.com

Printed in the United States of America

About the Author

Todd Kortemeier is a sportswriter, editor, and children's book author from Minneapolis. A devoted San Diego State basketball fan, he is thrilled to follow Kawhi Leonard's championship career in the NBA.

TABLE OF CONTENTS

HEAT
15
SPURS

1 YOUNG MVP

Kawhi Leonard caught a pass behind the three-point line. He made a move to get past Miami Heat guard Dwyane Wade. Then he used his right shoulder to shield the ball from Wade's reach.

As Leonard drove to the hoop, Chris Bosh stood in the way. Leonard drove his left shoulder into Bosh's chest. Then he tossed up a shot that dropped through the hoop. Bosh was called for a foul. Leonard sank the free throw for a three-point play.

Kawhi Leonard shows off his defensive skills against Miami in the 2014 NBA Finals.

Leonard beams as he discusses being named MVP of the NBA Finals in 2014.

It was Game 3 of the 2014 NBA Finals. The Heat and Leonard's San Antonio Spurs had split the first two games. Winning Game 3 would be a big boost toward winning the series.

In his third year in the NBA, Leonard was already a star on defense. But the Heat hadn't counted on Leonard becoming a superstar on offense, too. In Game 3, Leonard scored a team-high 29 points. The Spurs won 111–92. Then in Game 4, Leonard did it again. His 20 points led the way as San Antonio took control of the series with a 107–86 win.

The Spurs needed just one more win to clinch the NBA title. For the third game in a row, Leonard had the answer. He scored 22 points and added 10 rebounds. The Spurs closed out the series at home with a 104–87 victory.

Leonard was named the Most Valuable Player (MVP) of the series. He'd already proven he could play defense. But on the biggest stage of all, Leonard showed that he could be an offensive threat, too.

SURPRISE STAR

Leonard winning MVP was unexpected for a few reasons. He was only the sixth player ever to win Finals MVP without being an All-Star in the same season. And he was still just 22 years old, making him the third-youngest Finals MVP in NBA history.

KING
24

2 FIGHTING THROUGH TRAGEDY

Kawhi Anthony Leonard was born on June 29, 1991, in Riverside, California. He was the youngest of five kids and the only boy in his family. Kawhi grew up mostly at the home of his mother, Kim Robertson. But he learned basketball from his dad, Mark Leonard.

As a boy, Kawhi was obsessed with basketball. He watched *Come Fly with Me*, a movie about NBA superstar Michael Jordan, over and over again. Jordan was one of the greatest basketball players ever.

Kawhi goes up for a shot while playing for Martin Luther King High School in Riverside, California.

He was a superstar all over the world. But Kawhi didn't care about being famous. He just loved to play basketball.

Mark owned a car wash in Compton, California. Kawhi sometimes worked there as a kid. But tragedy struck when Kawhi was a junior in high school. On January 18, 2008, Mark was shot and killed while working at the car wash. Kawhi was devastated.

Basketball helped Kawhi get through the tragedy. It provided a distraction from his sadness. He even played a high school game the night after the shooting. After the game, he collapsed in tears. Kawhi struggled

PRO COUSIN

Kawhi's other sport growing up was football. His father always encouraged him to play both basketball and football. And football runs in the family. Kawhi's cousin is former NFL wide receiver Stevie Johnson. Johnson played in the NFL from 2008 to 2015, mostly with the Buffalo Bills.

Kawhi turned his hard work in high school into a scholarship to San Diego State.

on the court in the weeks that followed. But he wanted to make his father proud.

Kawhi came back the next year and had an incredible senior season. He averaged more than 22 points and 13 rebounds per game and led Martin Luther King High School to the state title game. He also was named Mr. Basketball in California as the best high school player in the state.

Some of the top college programs in the country offered Kawhi scholarships. Both USC and UCLA were recruiting him hard. And both were in his hometown. But a school to the south had reached out to him first.

San Diego State was a relatively small school on the college basketball scene. The Aztecs had reached the NCAA tournament five times but had never won a first-round game. They also had not produced many superstars. But even after other big-name schools came calling, Kawhi kept his word and stayed committed to San Diego State.

With Kawhi, the Aztecs had their best season ever. As a sophomore, Kawhi averaged 15.6 points and 10.6 rebounds per game.

After two years at San Diego State, Kawhi was ready for the NBA.

In the NCAA tournament, the Aztecs made a run to the Sweet 16 for the first time ever. Kawhi had proven he was ready for the jump to the highest level. He chose to skip his last two seasons of college basketball and enter the NBA Draft.

3 JOINING LEGENDS

For just a few hours, Kawhi Leonard was an Indiana Pacer. The Pacers had chosen him with the No. 15 pick in the 2011 NBA Draft. But Leonard was traded later that night. He was headed to San Antonio to join the Spurs.

The Spurs were a strong, veteran team. They had all-time great players in Tim Duncan and Tony Parker. They had a legendary coach in Gregg Popovich. Leonard was in a great situation with all the right people to guide him. But being

Leonard meets NBA commissioner David Stern before the trade between the Pacers and Spurs.

on a strong team also meant he didn't play as much as he was used to.

Leonard filled an important role for the Spurs. He played solid defense and provided some scoring. As he got to play more and more, Leonard's offensive game developed. After his breakout MVP performance in the 2014 NBA Finals, Leonard became a scoring machine.

In 2016, Leonard made his first All-Star Game. He averaged more than 20 points per game that season. He upped that to 25.5 in the 2016–17 season and made another All-Star Game. But Leonard's increased offensive skills did not mean his defense suffered. In fact, he was playing the best defense of his career.

Leonard contributed defense and hustle to a veteran Spurs roster.

Leonard was named NBA Defensive Player of the Year in 2015 and 2016.

The only thing going wrong for Leonard was injuries. He missed the end of the 2016–17 playoffs with an ankle injury. Then he was sidelined for the start of the 2017–18 season with a leg injury. Leonard came back to appear in a few games, but the injury lingered.

The injury caused other problems for Leonard and the Spurs. Leonard's personal doctors said the injury was too serious for him to play. But the team's doctors claimed Leonard was healthy enough to play.

THE KLAW

Leonard's nickname is "The Klaw." The name has two meanings. First, he's a great defender. He'll claw the ball away from an opposing player who is caught off guard. The name also refers to the size of Leonard's hands. They measure 11.25 inches (28.6 cm) from thumb to pinkie and are 9.75 inches (24.8 cm) long. His hands are 52 percent wider than the average man's hands.

Injuries kept Leonard (second from left) in street clothes for most of the 2017–18 season.

Rumors spread that Leonard's teammates were frustrated with him.

Leonard didn't play again that season. The bad feelings between him and the Spurs continued. Finally, Leonard requested a trade in the summer of 2018. He was looking for a fresh start and the chance to be a team leader.

SPALDING
RAPTORS
2
33
BLAZERS
9

4 LEADING THE NORTH

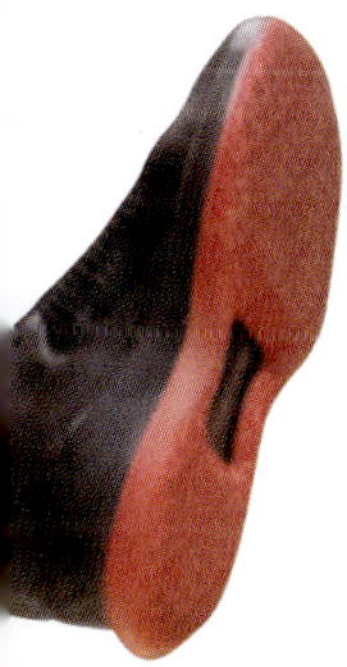

Few people expected Kawhi Leonard to go to the Toronto Raptors. But that's where he was traded in July 2018. The Raptors were a good team. But they had struggled to get over the hump. Most people assumed Leonard would leave as a free agent after one season.

Leonard's former team moved on without him. Spurs coach Gregg Popovich said that Leonard was not a team leader. But Leonard's Raptors teammates defended him. And the results spoke for

Leonard helped the Raptors get off to a flying start in 2018–19.

themselves. Leonard was having the best year of his career. And the Raptors started out 20–4, which was the best record in the NBA.

Toronto went 58–24 and won the Atlantic Division title. Leonard averaged 26.6 points and 7.3 rebounds per game, both career highs. The Raptors cruised into the 2019 NBA playoffs looking for their first title.

Then Leonard upped his game even more. Toronto easily topped the Orlando Magic in its opening playoff series. In the next round against Philadelphia, Leonard put up 45 points in Game 1. The series went back and forth before being decided by a seventh and final game. And it came down to the last second.

Leonard had the ball in a tie game. He dribbled to the corner and put up a three-point shot as time expired. The ball hit the rim

The Raptors survived a seven-game series with the 76ers to reach the Eastern Conference Finals.

and bounced. It bounced again. Then it bounced again, and again. And then it rolled in. The Raptors won the series. Leonard was the first player to win a Game 7 on a buzzer-beater.

BOUNCING BUZZER-BEATER

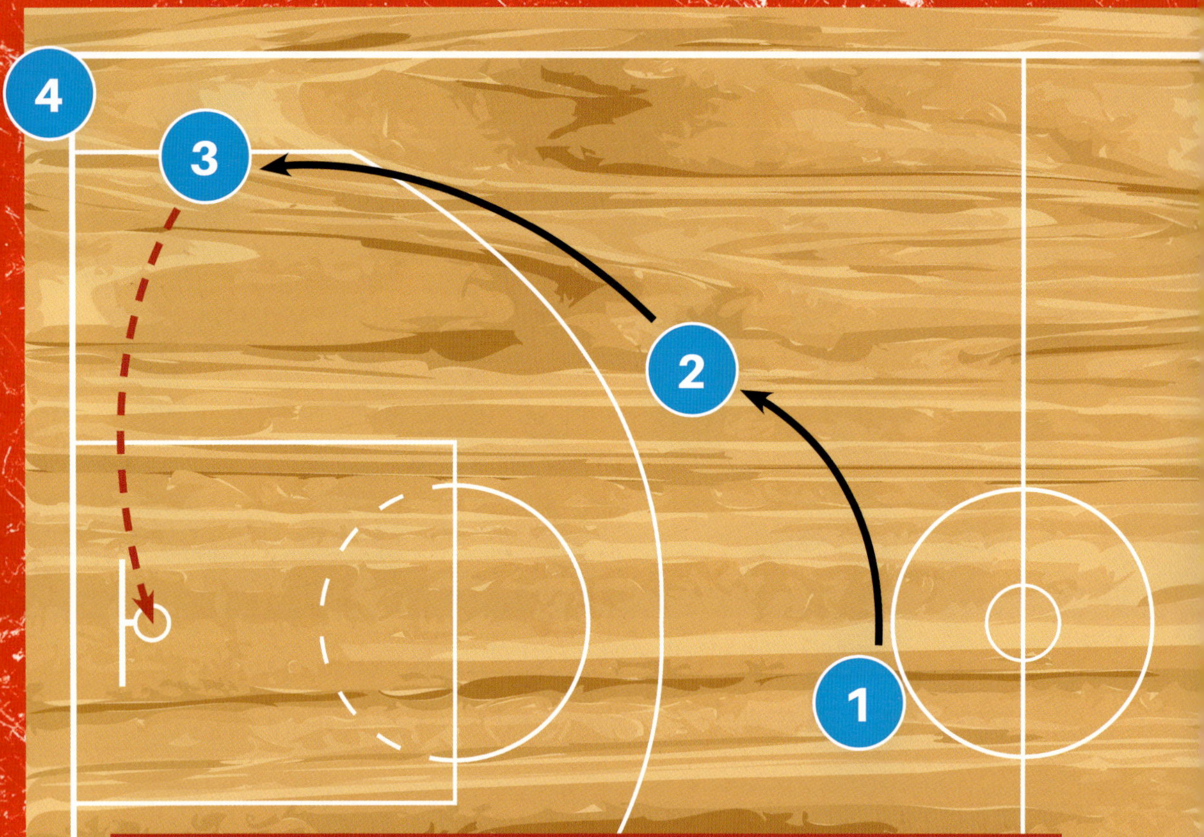

1. Leonard takes a pass from Marc Gasol and begins dribbling to his right.
2. He gets past Ben Simmons and is met by Joel Embiid.
3. Leonard launches the shot over the 7-foot Embiid.
4. After watching the ball bounce on the rim four times before dropping in, Leonard is mobbed by fans and teammates.

Leonard's buzzer-beating shot in Game 7 of the Eastern Conference semifinals had Raptors fans on the edge of their seats. The ball bounced on the rim four times before falling through the hoop to win the game.

AMONG GREATNESS

Only a handful of players have won two NBA Finals MVP awards. But even fewer have done it with two different teams. Leonard is only the third in history. The other two are legendary players. Kareem Abdul-Jabbar was the first. LeBron James was the second.

Suddenly, it seemed like the Raptors could do something special. But they lost the first two games of the Eastern Conference Finals against the Milwaukee Bucks. Leonard led the comeback, leading his team in scoring in three of the next four games. Toronto won four games straight to reach the first NBA Finals in team history.

The Raptors' opponent was a dynasty. The Golden State Warriors were going for their third championship in a row. And they almost never lost at home in the playoffs. But Leonard helped the Raptors turn that around. They won all three games on the Warriors' home court.

Leonard did what had never been done before—he brought an NBA championship to Canada.

Toronto clinched the series on the road in Game 6. Leonard scored 22 points as the Raptors won their first NBA championship. And Leonard was named the NBA Finals MVP for the second time. Leonard had done it again. He had led his team to the NBA championship. And at age 27, there was still plenty for him to achieve in the future.

TIMELINE

1. **Riverside, California (June 29, 1991)**
   Kawhi Leonard is born.

2. **San Diego, California (November 14, 2009)**
   Leonard plays his first college basketball game for the San Diego State Aztecs.

3. **Newark, New Jersey (June 23, 2011)**
   Leonard is chosen 15th overall in the NBA Draft by the Indiana Pacers, who immediately trade him to the San Antonio Spurs.

4. **San Antonio, Texas (December 26, 2011)**
   Leonard makes his NBA debut with the Spurs in a win over the Memphis Grizzlies.

5. **Miami, Florida (June 10, 2014)**
   Leonard scores 29 points in Game 3 of the NBA Finals. The Spurs go on to win the series in five games, and Leonard is named Finals MVP.

6. **Toronto, Ontario (October 17, 2018)**
   In his first game with the Toronto Raptors, Leonard scores 24 points and grabs 12 rebounds in a 116–104 win over Cleveland.

7. **Oakland, California (June 13, 2019)**
   Leonard wins his second NBA Finals MVP and Toronto wins its first NBA championship with a Game 6 victory over the Golden State Warriors.

MAP

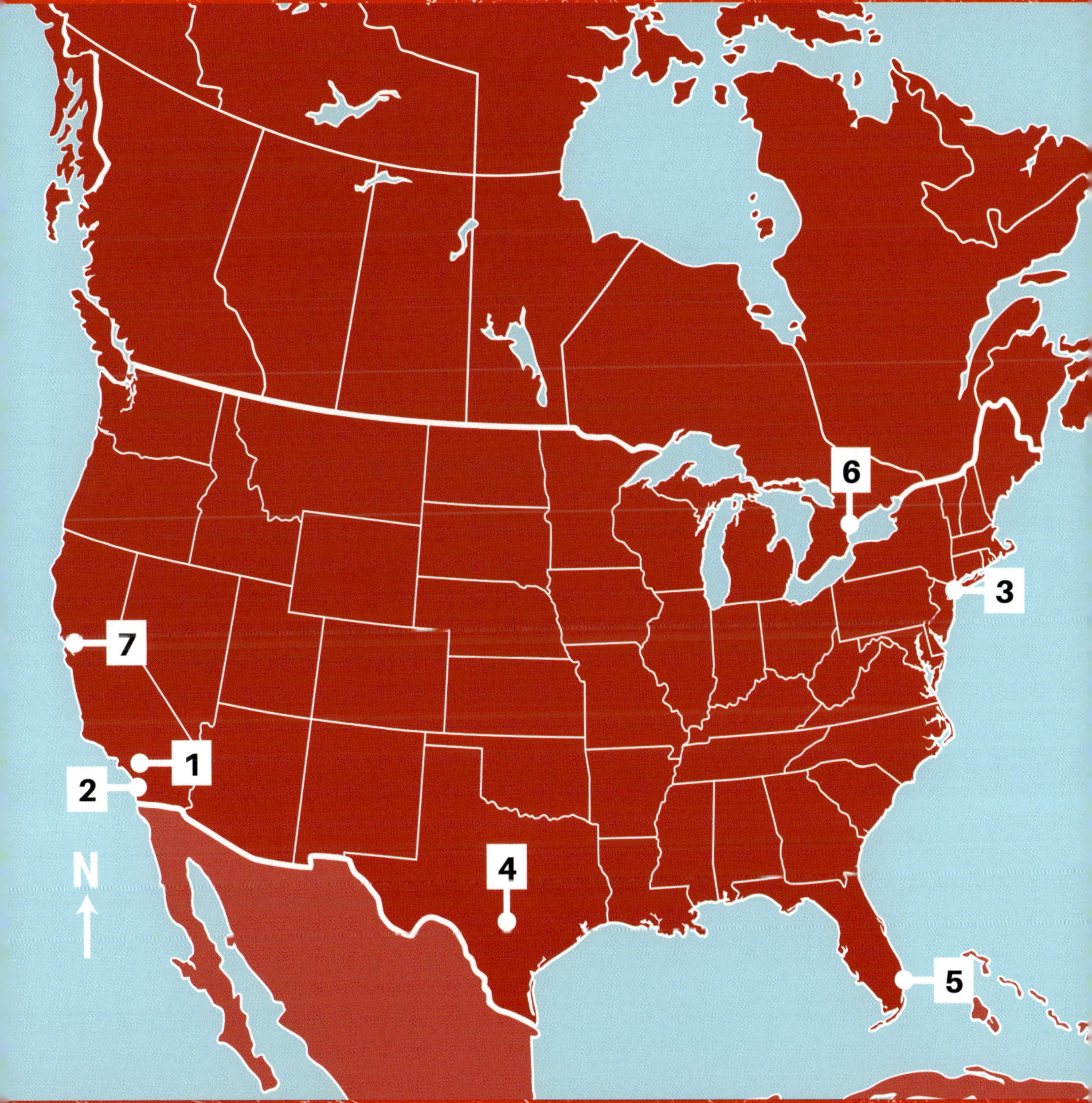

AT-A-GLANCE

Birth date: June 29, 1991

Birthplace: Riverside, California

Position: Small forward

Shoots: Right

Size: 6 feet 7 inches, 230 pounds

Current team: Toronto Raptors (2018–)

Past teams: San Diego State Aztecs (2009–11), San Antonio Spurs (2011–18)

Major awards: NBA champion (2014, 2019), NBA Finals MVP (2014, 2019), NBA Defensive Player of the Year (2015, 2016), NBA All-Star (2016, 2017, 2019)

Accurate through the 2018–19 season.

GLOSSARY

breakout
A significant early performance that is a sign of things to come.

buzzer-beater
A shot that is released before time has expired and goes through the hoop after time has expired.

conference
In the NBA, one of two groups that each contain half the league's teams.

division
A smaller group of teams that compete within a larger league.

draft
An event that allows teams to choose new players coming into the league.

dynasty
A team that has an extended period of success, usually winning multiple championships in the process.

free agent
A player whose rights are not owned by any team.

scholarship
Money awarded to a student-athlete to pay for educational expenses.

Sweet 16
The final 16 teams remaining in the annual NCAA basketball tournament.

veteran
A player who has played many years.

TO LEARN MORE

Books

Anderson, Josh, and Heather Kissock. *Toronto Raptors*. New York: AV2 by Weigl, 2016.

Fishman, Jon M. *Kawhi Leonard*. Minneapolis: Lerner Publications, 2018.

Schaller, Bob, with Dave Harnish. *The Everything Kids' Basketball Book: The All-Time Greats, Legendary Teams, Today's Superstars—and Tips on Playing Like a Pro*. New York: Adams Media, 2017.

Websites

Leonard's College Stats
www.sports-reference.com/cbb/players/kawhi-leonard-1.html

Leonard's NBA Bio
www.nba.com/players/kawhi/leonard/202695

Leonard's NBA Stats
www.basketball-reference.com/players/l/leonaka01.html

INDEX